I0814721

Kitchen
Killaz

KITCHEN VILLAIN

Feeding Curiosity

Killer Recipes to Satisfy Your Appetite for Instruction

Volume One

Chef Dane Brevoort

Feeding Curiosity: Killer Recipes to Satisfy Your Appetite for Instruction

Published by Clovercroft Publishing, Franklin, Tennessee
ClovercroftPublishingGroup.com

Cover and Interior Design by Billy Floyd

Printed in the United States of America

ISBN: 978-1-956370-68-3 (print)

FEEDING CURIOSITY

Killer Recipes to Satisfy Your Appetite for Instruction

Watermelon Salad.. 1
Crème Anglaise.. 3
Potato Leek Soup.. 7
Miso Honey Chicken.. 9
Chimichurri Street Tacos.. 13
Grilled Elote.. 15
Espresso Pork Sliders.. 19
Chicken Pot Stickers.. 21
Smoked Turkey Loaf.. 27
Papa's J's Grilled Pork Loin.. 29
Teriyaki Bourbon Burger.. 33
Bourbon Bacon Jam.. 37
Glossary of Terms.. 38
About the Chef.. 39
Bromance.. 40
Acknowledgements.. 41
Marketing.. 42

WATERMELON SALAD

This summer dish draws its inspiration from a harmonious blend of flavors that I believed would complement each other beautifully. It has consistently been a refreshing and sweet staple for my family and me during the peak heat of Florida summers.

The dish features feta cheese, which introduces a delicate, salty creaminess, paired with a balsamic reduction that offers a balanced sweetness that accentuates the freshness of the watermelon. This combination truly elevates the dish.

It is a quick and delightful recipe that pairs excellently with various summer activities, including cookouts, social gatherings, and outdoor adventures.

Watermelon Salad

with balsamic reduction

 8 servings  20 minutes

INGREDIENTS

Watermelon Salad:

1 Watermelon
1/2 - Red Onion (Julienne)
1/2 - English Cucumber (Chopped)
1 Cup - Feta Cheese
1/2 Cup - Walnuts (Crushed)
Spring Mix

For Reduction Sauce:

1 Cup - Balsamic Vinegar
1 Tablespoon - Sugar

DIRECTIONS

1. To make Balsamic reduction: Combine balsamic vinegar and sugar and whisk in a small sauté pan until blended
2. Reduce mixture on low heat for 10 minutes until nappe (coats and clings to a spoon), remove from heat and set aside
3. Remove skin from watermelon and cut into 1-inch pieces
4. Julienne onions, chop cucumber (large dice)
5. Plate watermelon cubes over bed of spring mix, add cucumber, onion, feta and walnuts then lightly drizzle balsamic reduction

CRÈME ANGLAISE

This dish serves as an excellent teaching tool for my advanced culinary students, particularly in mastering the technique of tempering. It underscores the principle that not all dishes require a multitude of ingredients to be exquisite; here, simplicity reigns supreme.

Composed of fewer than ten ingredients, this dessert skillfully balances the fresh, vibrant flavors of fruit and the aromatic richness of fresh vanilla bean. The addition of pirouette cookies introduces a delightful crunch, enhancing the overall texture and flavor profile with meticulous precision.

Designed as a light and sweet dessert, this dish is particularly suited for the summer months, offering a refreshing respite to cool the palate and delight the taste buds.

Crème Anglaise

English Cream

 4 servings  50 minutes

INGREDIENTS

Creme Anglaise:

1 Cup - Heavy Cream
1 Tbsp - Vanilla Bean OR
2Tbsp - Vanilla Extract (Pure)
5 Egg Yolks
1/2 Cup - Sugar

For Garnish:

1 Cup - Strawberries (Quartered)
1/2 Cup - Blueberries
Mint (Chiffonade)
3-4 Pirouette Cookies (Chopped)

DIRECTIONS

1. Split vanilla bean lengthwise down the center, using a butter knife carefully scrape the vanilla bean pulp and put it into a small container
2. In a small saucepan heat the heavy cream and bring it to a simmer, add vanilla pulp and stir until blended
3. In a small bowl, mix egg yolks and sugar until blended
4. Slowly pour 1/2 cup of warm cream into the egg mixture stirring constantly until incorporated
5. Slowly combine egg and cream mixture into the remaining cream on low heat, stirring constantly until thickened
6. Pour Anglaise mixture into serving bowls evenly then let refrigerate for 20 minutes
7. While cooling prepare your garnishes: rinse and quarter strawberries, rinse blueberries, chop pirouettes and chiffonade mint
8. Remove Creme Anglaise from the fridge, top with garnish, serve and enjoy!

July 7th, 2017

KITCHENKILLAZ

What is KitchenKillaz?

kitch·en
/ˈkiCH(ə)n/ - a room or area where food is prepared and cooked.

kill·er
/ˈkilər/ - a person or thing that kills..

kitch·enkill·a
/ˈkiCH(ə)n/ /ˈkilər/ - a person or thing that kills kitchens

KitchenKillaz is classified as an acoustic project crashing kitchens around the country. What started as a fun way to connect with our friends and family on a Friday night, has turned into an 8-year-long project which has brought us state to state and connected us to the world.

300+ kitchens later, and we're still at it.

Quite simply, we perform music LIVE in your kitchen to a crowd of your friends and family, while broadcasting our show across the interwebs. We focus on bringing the music and culinary communities together to introduce our audience to different people and world cultures.

Before they were the KitchenKillaz, they were just Billy Floyd & The Commodore, serenading viewers with a nightly song from various corners of their home. They played everywhere—the band room, the studio, and yes, even the bathroom, though that one thankfully never took off.

Then, one magical Friday night, they set up in the kitchen. Instantly, it was a hit. Viewership skyrocketed, comments flooded in, and the song requests kept coming for nearly two hours. By the show's end, they'd played their entire repertoire twice over, and the audience was clamoring for more.

In that moment, Billy and The Commodore knew they'd stumbled onto something special.

The following week was filled with exciting discussions about their future. One thing was crystal clear: They would be live again next Friday. And the kitchen? It was set to become their stage, and become their stage, it did.

During a vibrant two-hour show buzzing with both covers and originals, the airwaves came alive when Tim Haggard, a fellow musician and dear friend, tuned in. His words rang out clear: "I've seen you guys rock the studio and the band room, but now, you're absolutely slaying it in the kitchen. You guys are like KitchenKillers!" And just like that, in that spark of an instant, KitchenKillaz was born.

POTATO LEEK SOUP

Over the past three years, I have dedicated myself to designing and refining this soup recipe. It's a straightforward yet hearty autumn dish that is distinctly enhanced by the inclusion of bourbon bacon jam—a delightful addition we'll explore shortly.

This recipe is accessible enough for a culinary beginner to achieve with ease, yet the finished product offers a unique, complex, and immensely satisfying experience.

As an enthusiastic soup lover, my aim was to create a comforting dish perfect for savoring on a crisp fall evening, which, in Florida, can sometimes be a rare pleasure.

If it's a main course you're looking for, try this soup in a toasted bread bowl, creating a fulfilling and soul-satisfying meal.

Potato Leek Soup

 6 servings  50 minutes

INGREDIENTS

4 Tbsp - Butter (unsalted)
3 - Leeks, Chopped
(white and light green parts only)
4 - Garlic Cloves (Chopped)
2lbs. - Potatoes
(peeled, chopped into 1" pieces)
5 Cups - Chicken Stock
2 Bay Leaves
1 Tbsp - Thyme (dried)
1 1/2 Tsp - Salt
1/2 Tsp - Black Pepper
1 1/4 Cups - Heavy Cream

DIRECTIONS

1. Melt butter in stock pot over medium heat
2. Add leeks and garlic, stir regularly until leeks are soft
3. Add potatoes, stock, bay leaves, thyme, salt and pepper to pot and bring it to a boil
4. Cover stock pot with lid, turn heat to low and let simmer for 20 minutes until potatoes are fork tender
5. Turn off heat, and remove bay leaves
6. Puree ingredients using a hand-held immersion blender (stick-blender)
7. Add heavy cream and bring back to a simmer, stirring until thickened
8. Serve with infused chive oil and bacon jam, Enjoy!

MISO-HONEY CHICKEN

By the age of 20, I had ascended to the role of Sous-Chef at Delta Phi Epsilon Sorority, where I had the privilege of preparing meals for 186 members, serving three meals daily, five days a week. Under the mentorship of the Executive Chef, I was encouraged to infuse the menu with my unique culinary perspective.

During my tenure of five years at Delta Phi Epsilon, we collaborated on numerous meal plans. Notably, my Miso-Chicken dish became a beloved regular feature. This period was foundational in my culinary career, offering a profound education in kitchen management, menu development, and dish creation, all of which have been instrumental in my professional growth as a chef.

This experience remains deeply cherished, a significant cornerstone in my journey in the culinary arts.

Miso-Honey Chicken

 6 servings  45 minutes

INGREDIENTS

6 Chicken Breasts (Pounded Thin)
1/2 Cup - All Purpose Flour
1/2 Tablespoon - Salt
1 Teaspoon - Black Pepper
1/2 Teaspoon - Garlic Powder
1/4 Cup - Vegetable Oil (divided)
For Miso Sauce:
4 Cups - Chicken Stock
8 oz. - Red Miso Paste
3/4 Cup - Honey
1 Tablespoon - Lime Juice
1 Tablespoon - Cilantro (Finely Chopped)
1 Teaspoon - Lemon Grass (Minced)

For Slurry:

1 Tablespoon Cornstarch
1/4 Cup - Water

For Garnish:

1 Red Onion - Thinly Sliced
1 Bunch Green Onion (Scallions) - Sliced Thin on Bias

DIRECTIONS

1. Trim fat off the chicken breast, and use a meat mallet to pound the chicken evenly
2. In a medium bowl mix flour, salt, pepper, and garlic powder, dredge chicken in the seasoned flour until coated, shake off excess, and set aside
3. In a medium saucepan add chicken stock, miso paste, and honey. Whisk until blended and smooth
4. Add lime juice, cilantro, and lemongrass. Then turn on the heat to med-low and bring to a simmer stirring periodically
5. Add slurry to thicken the sauce to create a nappe consistency
6. Prepare garnish and set aside
7. In two large saute pans add vegetable oil (1/8 cup per pan), turn the heat to med-low
8. Pan-sear the chicken on each side until a light golden brown to an internal temperature of 165 degrees
9. Reduce heat to low and add 1 cup of miso sauce to each pan and let reduce by half
10. Add 1/4 of the red onion and 1/4 cup scallions to the pan, let simmer for 5 minutes then turn off the heat
11. Serve with cilantro rice and sauteed bok choy, Enjoy!

KITCHENKILLAZ

Over the years, our musical journey crisscrossed Florida, bringing us into the welcoming kitchens of incredible homes and restaurants—from the shores of Okeechobee to the bustling streets of Port Saint Lucie, and from the vibrant scenes of Ft. Lauderdale and beyond. This adventure allowed us to forge deep connections with wonderful families and indulge in the rich, diverse flavors of Florida's culinary landscape.

Along the way, we teamed up with talented artists like Josh Bauer, Brian Demeter, and Anthony Hernandez. Friends and family often joined us on Friday nights, turning each kitchen into a stage for singing and dancing our hearts out.

Our shared experiences have ranged from savoring arepas to discovering halushka, but perhaps none so memorable as the first time we all sang in chorus, celebrating the quirky yet beloved combo of Pop-Tarts & Butter.

These moments wove us tightly together. For one hour each week, we set aside our troubles, paused our frustrations, and united under the banners of music, community, and cuisine—a triumphant trio that has become the cornerstone of our project.

We've been fortunate enough to call a few places home, and our community has been there to support us each time. We've opened our house on many Friday nights, packed the kitchen, and filled the air with laughter, singing, made-up websites, funny stories, and the aroma of delicious foods.

These gatherings are a way to present our music, meet new friends, make new memories, and book new kitchens. We've celebrated birthdays, anniversaries, engagements, house warmings, and homecomings in the heart of our very own humble abode, but we found community in those hosts and kitchens that invited us into theirs.

CHIMICHURRI STREET TACOS

Tacos are my love language and I guarantee you'll fall in love with these.

These tacos are simple to prepare and a delight to enjoy. I initially shared this straightforward recipe with my son when he was 10 years old. It has since found itself in heavy rotation in my home, being prepared for my wife and me during our family board game or movie nights.

A key component of this dish is the chimichurri sauce, which we use extensively. It serves not only as a marinade for the steak but also as an exquisite cilantro-infused topping for the tacos.

For those seeking a spicier twist, consider substituting serrano and jalapeño peppers with habaneros. Adding these fiery peppers will elevate your experience to what I like to call 'taco heaven.'

Street Tacos

 12 -15 Tacos  95 minutes

INGREDIENTS

2 lb. - Flank Steak (remove silverskin)

Chimichurri Sauce:

1 Cup - Olive Oil
3/4 Cup - Red Wine Vinegar
2 Jalapeños (chopped)
1 Serrano (chopped)
5 Cloves - Garlic (peeled)
1 Shallot (peeled and chopped)
1 Bunch - Cilantro (no stems)
1 Bunch - Parsley (no stems)
2 Tbsp - Oregano (fresh)
1 1/2 Tsp - Salt

Garnish for Tacos:

4 Plum Tomatoes - Brunoised Cut
1 Red Onion (small) - Julienne
Cut Cotija Cheese - (crumbled)

For Shells:

1 Package - Flour Tortilla Shells (small)
2 Tablespoons - Butter (unsalted)
1 Tablespoon - Olive Oil

DIRECTIONS

1. Remove fat and silverskin from steak and set aside in large bowl
2. In a medium bowl add chimichurri ingredients, blend with immersion (stick) until smooth
3. Pour 1 cup of the Chimichurri sauce over the steak. Marinate in the refrigerator for 1 hour, saving the remaining sauce to add to the tacos
4. Prepare your garnish by crumbling the cotija cheese, julienning the onion & brunoise the tomatoes. Set aside in individual containers
5. Grill marinated steak to desired temperature (135° for med rare), take off grill and let rest for 5 minutes
6. To prepare taco shells lightly brown one side of flour tortillas in butter and oil on medium low heat, once done remove and place in taco holders
7. Slice steak thinly against the grain and place slices into the tortilla shells
8. Garnish taocs by adding a spoonful of chimichurri sauce, cotija cheese, onion slices, tomatos and Enjoy!

ELOTE (MEXICAN STREET CORN)

As you indulge in the delights of taco heaven, be sure to reserve some room on your plate for this boldly flavored side dish.

Street corn, a staple found at farmers' markets, food truck rallies, fairs, and festivals, is transformed in this recipe, which puts a unique twist on the traditional "elote."

Replacing the tangy zest of tajin, I have incorporated paprika and chipotle powder, lending a spicy kick that is atypical of conventional street corn.

Char-grilling these ears of corn introduces an additional layer of smoky flavor, enhancing each of the individual ingredients that complete this culinary journey to taco heaven.

Grilled Elote
Street Corn

 4 servings  20 minutes

INGREDIENTS

4 - Ears of Corn
1/2 Cup - Sour Cream
1/2 Cup - Mayonnaise
5 Cloves - Garlic (Minced)
Zest and Juice of 1 Lime
2 Tbps - Cilantro (Chopped Fine)
1/4 Tsp - Chipotle Chili Powder
1/4 Tsp - Smoked Paprika
Salt - To Taste
1/2 Cup - Cotija Cheese (Crumbled)

DIRECTIONS

1. Shuck corn (if necessary) and be sure to remove all fibrous pieces from corn cob
2. Fill a medium stock pot with water, cover with a lid, and bring to a boil
3. Lower heat to a simmer and boil corn for 8-10 minutes until tender
4. Turn off the heat, remove the corn, and set aside
5. In a medium bowl combine sour cream and mayo
6. Zest and juice lime into the bowl and stir until combined
7. Add chopped cilantro, salt and spices
8. Stir until all ingredients are combined
9. Brush mixture onto corn until thoroughly coated
10. Grill corn for 5 minutes, turn corn to ensure each side is cooked
11. Remove corn from grill and lightly brush remaining sauce onto corn while corn is warm
12. Garnish with Cotija cheese, paprika, and chopped cilantro, Enjoy!

Over the past seven seasons, our home studio has transformed into a vibrant hub where cooks, creators, and chefs converge to share their culinary secrets with the world. Our kitchen has buzzed with the energy of friends and family, all gathering to infuse our space with love and positivity while we explore and showcase diverse recipes and ingredients from across the globe. This melting pot of passions brings us together, fostering a shared enthusiasm that resonates through each episode.

Our journey has taken us all over the sunny expanses of Florida, stepping into the kitchens of families, friends, and neighbors. We've exchanged handshakes with innovative creators and sampled a world of flavors—from appetizers to desserts. We've been privileged not just to taste these divine creations but also to share the rich culture and heritage behind each dish with viewers worldwide.

From the Irish inspirations of Chef Michael O'Brien and the Guyanese specialties of Christina Gopaul to the traditional Dominican dishes from Leinny "Luscious" Lerner, we've relished a tapestry of tastes that are as rare as they are delightful.

Our platform is a fun, welcoming stage for anyone eager to share their passion, whatever it may be. We cherish and support all kinds of passions, believing that the joy of creation is meant to be shared far and wide.

KitchenKillaz has rocked out with some amazing talents, including Tampa's own Chef Erik Youngs, "The VooDoo Chef." As a major supporter, he's crashed our kitchen, asked us to crash his, and even invited us to perform live on the VooDoo Chef Foundation float at the Gasparilla Pirate Parade.

His commitment to culinary education shines through the VooDoo Chef Foundation in Hillsborough County, which offers grants and scholarships to aspiring chefs, helping them forge promising careers through higher education.

Discover more at: www.voodoocheffoundation.com/

ESPRESSO PORK SLIDERS

Featured on KitchenKillaz, this recipe marked my debut culinary presentation to an eager audience.

These sliders draw inspiration from "VooDoo Dirt," a seasoning blend available at voodoochef.com. My aim was to harmonize the seasoning's sweet profile, characterized by espresso and brown sugar, with a Jicama slaw—a recipe I developed during my time as a culinary student in college.

The rich earthiness of the espresso rub perfectly complements the tenderness of the ground pork, and is exquisitely balanced by the crispness of the apple in the Jicama slaw.

Set this deliciousness inside a butter-toasted bun and you have some of the most savory sliders this side of the Mississippi.

Espresso Pork Sliders
with Jicama Apple Slaw

 8 sliders  30 minutes

INGREDIENTS

1 lb. Ground Pork
1 Pack - Slider Buns

For Espresso Rub:

4 Tablespoons - Espresso
2 Tablespoon - Brown Sugar
1Teaspoon - Salt
1 Teaspoon - Black Pepper
1 Teaspoon - Garlic Powder
1 Teaspoon - Onion Powder
1 Teaspoon - Paprika
1/4 Teaspoon - Cayenne Pepper

For Slaw:

1 Green Apple (Batonnet)
1 Jicama Root (Batonnet)
1/4 Red Cabbage (Shredded)
1/4 Green Cabbage (Shredded)
1 Tablespoon - Cilantro

Slaw Dressing:

3/4 Cup - Mayo
1 Tablespoon - Sugar
1 Teaspoon - White Wine Vinegar
1 Teaspoon - Pineapple Juice
1 Teaspoon - Hot Sauce

DIRECTIONS

1. Mold ground pork into 2 oz patties cover with plastic wrap and refrigerate until ready to season
2. In a small bowl mix ingredients for rub and set aside
3. In another small bowl whisk mayonnaise, white wine vinegar, hot sauce and sugar together to make slaw dressing
4. Shred the cabbage into 1 inch ribbons and place in a medium bowl
5. Peel jicama and apple, then slice and cut them into batonnet cuts (1/4 in. x 1/4 in. x 1 in.) and add it to the cabbage
6. Finely chop cilantro and mix it into the cabbage bowl
7. Add the dressing to the cabbage bowl and mix together until the contents are coated
8. Remove pork from refrigerator and season each side of the sliders evenly
9. Add 1 tbsp of oil a saute pan and heat up pan
10. Sear pork on each side until an internal temperature of 155 degrees is reached
11. Serve pork slider over slaw and toasted bun, Enjoy!

CHICKEN POT STICKERS

These delights scarcely last five minutes in my home, so I recommend setting a few aside before presenting them to your guests. This sweet and crispy treat is not only crunchy and satisfying but also serves as a healthier alternative to traditional fried amuse-bouche.

The true standout of this dish is the apricot jam, which elevates the already delightful pot sticker to new heights, making it a favorite at any gathering, party, or event.

Chicken Pot Stickers

 15 servings  90 minutes

INGREDIENTS

2 lbs. Ground Chicken
2 Tbsp. - Garlic (minced)
1 Tbsp. - Ginger (minced)
1/2 Cup - Soy
1 Tsp Sesame Oil
1 Tsp - Crushed Red Pepper
1 - Red Pepper (Brunoise)
2 - Carrots (grated)
1lb Head - Napa Cabbage (shredded)

DIRECTIONS

1. In a large sauté pan cook ground chicken thoroughly to 165 degrees on medium heat
2. Drain off excess liquid, and put pan back over heat
3. Add minced garlic and ginger and sauté until fragrant
4. Add soy, sesame oil and crushed red pepper. Mix in pan and cook on low heat until liquid has evaporated.
5. Turn off heat, let chicken cool and set aside
6. remove seeds and brunoise red pepper, peel and grate carrots, and shred cabbage
7. Add cooled chicken and vegetables together into a large bowl and set aside
8. To make egg wash, crack two eggs into a small container, add 2 tablespoons of water and whisk until blended
9. Lay 2-3 wonton wrappers out at a time on a cutting board, using a basting brush or your finger coat the outer edge of the wonton wrappers with egg wash
10. Place approx.. 1/2 oz. of chicken mixture onto center of wonton wrapper and fold it diagonally making sure not to tear wrapper sealing it shut
11. Repeat until all wrappers are stuffed, place on a sheet pan a cover with a damp paper towel, until ready to cook

Continued on next page...

Chicken Pot Stickers

 15 servings  90 minutes

INGREDIENTS

For Apricot Teriyaki Glaze:

1 - 18 oz Jar Apricot Preserves
1 Cup - Water
4 Tbsp. - Soy
2 Tbsp. - Sriracha
1 Tsp - Lime Juice
4 - Garlic Cloves (smashed)
1/2 Tbsp. - Ginger (peeled and chopped)
1 Stalk - Scallion (Chopped)

1 Package Wonton Wrappers
2 - Eggs
Vegetable Oil - For pan frying
(enough to coat bottom of pan)

Garnish:

Sesame Seeds
1/2 Cup - Scallions (Sliced)

DIRECTIONS

To make Apricot Sauce:

1) In a medium sauce pan add apricot preserves, water, sriracha, and lime juice. Whisk together until blended and bring to a simmer
2) Add garlic, ginger and scallions, reduce heat to low and let sauce reduce by half or until desired consistency

To Fry Pot Stickers:

1. In a large sauté pan add enough oil to coat the bottom and turn heat to medium
2. Working in batches, pan sear each pot sticker until golden brown
3. Place cooked pot stickers into bowl, add apricot sauce and toss pot stickers until coated.
4. Serve shingled on a plate, top with scallions and sesame seeds, Enjoy!

CHEF'S NOTE

Crafting this recipe is a true labor of love, requiring patience and meticulous attention to detail. Embrace each step with care and cherish the process of bringing these flavors to life.

The ingredients blend harmoniously to create a dish that is not only a feast for the palate but also a celebration of culinary passion. As you mix, season, and simmer, allow yourself to be immersed in the experience, noting the transformation of simple ingredients into something extraordinary.

This is a dish best enjoyed slowly, ensuring every nuance of flavor is savored. However, be prepared: once presented, these delights are surely to be swiftly consumed by eager guests. So, take a moment to appreciate your handiwork before it vanishes from the plate, leaving behind only the memory of a meal made with devotion.

LIVE 13:31

KITCHENKILLAZ

At KitchenKillaz, we celebrate creativity in all its forms, providing a vibrant and positive space for everyone passionate about their crafts to share them with the world. Every month, we host "Community Conversations," inviting creators from all walks of life to join us on the show and explore what truly inspires them.

Whether you're a production company, actor, cosplayer, musician, or even a butcher, baker, or candlestick maker—our platform is for you. If you have a drive, a passion, our show is your stage. Our community is incredibly supportive, always ready to engage, motivate, and celebrate the diverse talents of our guests. Join us and let's make magic together!

Find out more at: www.kitchenkillaz.com

KITCHENKILLAZ

KitchenKillaz thrives on community, a cornerstone of our identity. We're all about gathering people to celebrate life and passion, sparking friendships and connections that nurture our social fabric, bringing together people and businesses that drive progress.

Our door is open to all—chefs, cooks, students, and anyone who revels in the joy of life and love. We're dedicated to maintaining a vibrant, positive atmosphere for everyone.

Our musical journey spans decades and genres, weaving tales of love, sacrifice, and success that resonate globally. We pay tribute to the musical legends who inspire us and strive to craft songs that move and inspire others.

At the heart of KitchenKillaz are three ingredients: music, culinary, and community. For over 7 years, we've stayed true to our message and values, crafting a recipe for success that's as sincere as it is effective.

We're a touring acoustic project crashing kitchens around the country.
We do it on Fridays & we do it for free.

SMOKED TURKEY LOAF

This dish originated from a challenge posed by Tyler Garretson—a "Meatloaf" challenge to be precise.

Tyler entered the contest with a confident recipe, aspiring to earn the title of "The Meatloaf Master."

Challenge accepted.

I started by blending the rich flavors of turkey with the savory notes of Italian sausage, enhanced by the homestyle heartiness of chicken stock.

To this base, I added the traditional "Cajun Trinity" of bell peppers, white onions, and celery. This was complemented by thyme and garlic, then smoked over hickory wood and crowned with my signature bacon jam.

Spoiler Alert: I won. Love you, Tyler. ;-)

Smoked Turkey Loaf

 8 servings  70 minutes

INGREDIENTS

3lbs. - Ground Turkey
1lb. - Ground Mild Italian Sausage
1 Egg
1/2 Cup - Bread Crumbs
1/2 White Onion (Small Dice)
1/2 Green Pepper (Small Dice)
2 Stalks Celery (Small Dice)
3 Cloves Garlic (Minced)
1 Tbsp - Thyme (Dried)
2 Tsp - Salt
1 Tsp - Black Pepper
1 Cup - Chicken Stock

DIRECTIONS

1. In a large bowl combine ground turkey and sausage
2. Add bread crumbs and egg
3. Add diced onion, green pepper, celery and garlic
4. Add thyme, salt and black pepper
5. Add chicken stock and mix by hand until combined evenly
6. Grease two loaf pans with cooking spray and place 1/2 of the mixture in each pan
7. Cook in the smoker at 325 degrees for 40-50 minutes until the internal temperature reaches 165 degrees
8. Remove from smoker and let rest 5-8 minutes
9. Serve 1/2-3/4 inch slices over your favorite mashed potato recipe and garnish with bacon jam, Enjoy!

PAPA JAY'S GRILLED PORK LOIN

Holiday feasts, graduation celebrations, Friday evenings, and college football barbecues—no matter the occasion, Jay was always prepared to present a meal that had everyone eagerly queuing for a second helping.

This family welcomed me and supported me throughout my high school years. It was in this nurturing environment that I discovered my passion for cooking while simultaneously learning the true essence of family.

This recipe serves as a tribute to the man who played a pivotal role in my upbringing, and it honors a dish he lovingly prepared for us on countless occasions, whether we were celebrating, supporting our favorite sports teams, or simply gathering as a family.

Papa Jay's Grilled Pork Loin

 8 servings  70 minutes

INGREDIENTS

1 Pork Tenderloin

For Marinade:

3/4 Cup - Olive Oil
1/4 Cup - Red Wine Vinegar
4 Cloves - Garlic (minced)
2 Tbsp - Sugar
1 Tbsp - Mustard
1 Tbsp - Worchestershire
2 Tsp - Soy
1 Tsp - Lemon Juice
1 Tsp - Oregano (dried)
1 Tsp - Basil (dried)
1 Tsp - Crushed Red Pepper
1/2 Tsp - Onion Powder
1 Tsp - Salt
1/2 Tsp - Black Pepper

DIRECTIONS

1. Trim fat and silverskin off of pork loin and set aside
2. In a medium-sized bowl incorporate and blend all ingredients for the marinade until emulsified
3. Add pork loin to the marinade and refrigerate for a minimum of 1 hour
4. Grill the pork loin and brush the remaining marinade onto the pork
5. Cook to an internal temperature of 145 degrees, then let rest for 5 minutes
6. To serve cut pork loin at an angle, Enjoy!

KITCHENKILLAZ

Every kitchen, every friend, chef, restaurant, family, tune, and adventure has brought us to this remarkable milestone in our journey. We've diligently nurtured relationships and are thrilled to be part of a vibrant network of individuals all dedicated to mastering their craft, capturing moments, and sharing them with the world.

We've invested our hearts into this project and are deeply grateful to everyone who has supported us along the way. Whether you've tuned into our broadcasts, welcomed us into your homes, created artwork, or introduced us to your loved ones, the success of KitchenKillaz is a collective triumph.

Within KitchenKillaz, there's an enduring sense of family. It travels with us into every host kitchen and permeates the air in ours—a warm, welcoming vibe filled with hugs, high-fives, laughter, and of course, scrumptious meals.

By purchasing this book and joining our community, you've done something truly wonderful. We are honored by your choice to embrace our story, learn more about us, and share in what we do.

Thank you immensely for your support.

To my buddy, Dane.

Thank you, brother. Thank you for all of your time, your love, and your friendship. Thank you for introducing me to your wonderful family, and for quickly becoming a part of mine. Thank you for your diligence and passion, the love for your craft, your drive to excel, and the constant education of those around you.

It was a true pleasure working with you on this project, and I look forward to many more adventures in our future. You inspire us all. You believe in us all, and your leadership and talent cannot be overstated. You've become a great friend, and I am truly blessed to have you in my life. You are a true "KitchenKilla"

Your Friend, Billy

TERIYAKI BOURBON BURGER

In the mystical realm of VooDooBash 2023, amidst a carnival of culinary wizards and their enchanting creations, a burger of legend was crafted—conceived in the crucible of fierce competition. Deftly, the creator infused this burger with a draught of creativity, a sprinkle of passion, and a commanding will to eclipse all rivals in the great burger-bash saga.

This was no ordinary burger; it was destined to rule them all!

Nestled within a toasted brioche throne, it bore layers of enchantment: a leaf of bibb lettuce, a tangy tapestry of pickled Daikon and carrot, a 6oz patty of 80/20 ground beef, grilled to perfection, cloaked in molten pepper-jack cheese, and crowned with braised pork belly bathed in a pineapple bourbon glaze.

The contest was formidable, the adversaries bold and valiant.

One burger rose to triumph.

Alas, it was not this burger.

But beware, VooDoo! For next time, the saga continues...

Teriyaki Bourbon Burger

 8 servings  120 minutes

INGREDIENTS

For Burgers:

2 lbs - Ground Beef
3 Garlic Cloves (Minced)
1/2 Tablespoon - Ginger (Minced)
1 Stalk - Scallion (Minced)
1 Tablespoon - Sriracha
Salt - To Taste
Black Pepper - To Taste

For Teriyaki Bourbon Glaze:

6 Garlic Gloves
1 Tbsp - Olive Oil
1 Cup - Pineapple Juice
1 1/2 Cup - Brown Sugar
1/3 Cup - Water
2/3 Cup - Teriyaki Sauce
3 Tbsp - Lime Juice
1/4 Tsp - Crushed Red Pepper
1/4 Cup - Bourbon

DIRECTIONS

For Burgers:

1. Place ground beef into a medium bowl, add minced garlic, ginger, scallion, and sriracha and mix until blended
2. Mold ground beef into 4-ounce patties, then salt and pepper both sides of the patties as desired
3. Grill burgers to 155 degrees and melt pepper jack cheese over the top of burger.

For Teriyaki Bourbon Glaze:

1. In a small sheet of foil place 6 cloves of garlic and drizzle 1 tablespoon of oil over them, fold the foil over the garlic sealing it shut, and bake in the oven for 15 minutes at 350 degrees until garlic is tender and fragrant
2. Remove garlic from the foil and place it into a medium saucepan, crush garlic in a pan with a fork until pulpy
3. Add remaining glaze ingredients to saucepan, and whisk until blended
4. Reduce sauce on medium heat whisking periodically until nappe
5. Remove from heat and set aside

Continued on next page...

Teriyaki Bourbon Burger

 8 servings  120 minutes

INGREDIENTS

For Do Chua:

1/2 lb. - Carrots (Peeled & Batonnet)
1/2 lb. - Daikon Radish (Peeled & Batonnet)
1/2 Cup and 2 Teaspoons - Sugar
1 Teaspoon - Salt
1 1/4 Cups - White Vinegar
1 Cup - Water
2 Tablespoons - Honey
1 Teaspoon - Crushed Red Pepper

DIRECTIONS

For Do Chua:

1. Peel carrots and Daikon then cut into batonnet and place into a small bowl
2. Coat Carrots and Daikon with 2 teaspoons of sugar and 1 teaspoon of salt, let it rest for 5 minutes
3. Rinse sugar off and put carrots and Daikon into a refrigerator-safe container with a lid
4. In a medium bowl whisk sugar, vinegar, water, honey, and crushed red pepper until blended, then pour mixture over carrots and Daikon, place in the refrigerator for an hour before serving

Continued on next page...

Teriyaki Bourbon Burger

 8 servings  120 minutes

INGREDIENTS

For Pork Belly:

1 lb. - Pork Belly

For Burger Build:

1. Over a toasted bun place lettuce then carrots and daikon
2. place the burger on top of the carrots and daikon
3. Top the burger with pork belly and extra sauce if desired
4. Skewer the top bun to hold the burger together, serve, and Enjoy!

DIRECTIONS

For Pork Belly:

1. Remove the top layer of skin and roughly cut pork belly and 1/2 inch pieces
2. Place pork belly into a pot and cover the pork with cold water, blanch pork for for 15 minutes on medium heat
3. Remove pork from liquid and pat dry with a paper towel (discard liquid)
4. Place pork into a hot oiled pan searing pork on all sides until golden brown
5. Reduce heat to low and add half of the teriyaki glaze to the pan, allow to simmer, and stir occasionally for 10 minutes. After 10 Minutes remove from heat and place a lid on saucepan to keep it warm

Bourbon Bacon Jam

 1.5 Cups  35 minutes

INGREDIENTS

1 lb. - Bacon (cut into 1/4 inch pieces)
1/2 White Onion, Small Dice
1 Shallot, Minced
3 Garlic Cloves, Minced
1/4 Cup - Brown Sugar
1/2 Cup - Maple Syrup
1/4 Cup - Apple Cider Vinegar
3 Tablespoons - Bourbon
1 Teaspoon - Chipotle Chili Powder

DIRECTIONS

1. In a large saute pan cook bacon pieces over medium heat until crispy
2. Transfer cooked bacon to a paper towel-lined plate reserving about 2 tablespoons of bacon fat in the pan
3. On medium-low heat, add onions and shallots, stirring often until onions are caramelized (about 5 minutes)
4. Deglaze pan with bourbon
5. Add garlic, brown sugar, maple syrup, apple cider vinegar, chili powder and cooked bacon
6. Bring mixture to a simmer then reduce heat to low.
7. Reduce until desired thickness (about 8-10 minutes)

GLOSSARY / TERMS

Brunoise: 1/8" x 1/8 "x 1/8"
(BROON-wahz)

Small : 1/4" x 1/4" x 1/4"

Medium: 1/2" x 1/2" x 1/2"

Large: 3/4" x 3/4" x 3/4"

Julienne : 1/8" x 1/8" x 1 -2" in length

Mince: Smaller than a brunoise: no precision needed

Dice: Cut foods into small 1/4" squares. Pieces should be as even as possible.

Batonnet: Rectangular stick measuring 1/2" × 1/2" x 2 1/2 to 3" length
(bah-tow -nay)

Chopped: No precision needed though make sure all cuts are roughly the same size

Temper: Slowly add a small amount of a hot liquid to a cooler ingredient while constantly stirring to avoid clumping or curdling.

ABOUT THE CHEF

Chef Dane Brevoort is a seasoned culinary professional with over two decades of experience. A Florida native, Chef Dane earned a Bachelor's degree in Hospitality Management from the University of Central Florida. He is renowned for his innovative use of Florida's fresh produce, skillfully infused into diverse cuisines.

Growing up in Gainesville, Chef Dane's passion for cooking was ignited by his father's nightly meals and family gatherings. He started his culinary career as a dishwasher, quickly advancing to banquet and line cook roles, where he helped prepare meals for the University of Florida football program. In 2005, he became the Sous Chef at the Delta Phi Epsilon Sorority, creating daily meals for its 186 members. His journey took him to Orlando in 2011, where he worked as a chef at several prestigious restaurants, including the Royal Pacific Resort.

Currently residing in Casselberry, Florida, Chef Dane is committed to educating the next generation of chefs as a Chef Instructor at a local high school. He also offers private catering for small events and private dining. Mentorship is his passion, guiding students to success in culinary competitions. His students' achievements include:

- 1st Place and People's Choice, 2024 Chili Competition
- 4th Place Overall, ProStart 2024
- 1st Place Edible Centerpiece, ProStart 2024
- 5th Place Hospitality Management, ProStart 2023
- 2nd Place Voodoo Underground 2023

In early 2024, the Seminole County Tourism Board honored Chef Dane for his significant contributions to the hospitality industry and the community.

"A BROMANCE FORGED IN BBQ, SMITHED BY A PIG JIG...
...BROUGHT TOGETHER WITH VOODOO AND BOUND IN FRIENDSHIP"

Chef Dane and Billy Floyd have become a dynamic duo of long-haired, slightly bearded men, the likes of which the world has never seen due to a chance of happenstance that occurred, on the morning of October 22nd in 2022. The earth experienced a seismic shift of emotion as hands were shaken, food and drinks were enjoyed, and a partnership was born.

They've rocked atop the VooDoo Foundation Gasparilla float, teamed up in the KitchenKillaz studio, many times, and become close friends. Their shared passion for music, culinary, community, and education has culminated in a creative expression of delicious instruction and a clear path to tantalized taste buds.

This cookbook has long been a topic of enthusiastic discussion within the KitchenKillaz community, and we are thrilled to see it come to life. It is designed to educate and inspire, featuring recipes ranging from the straightforward to the sophisticated, all intended to infuse the kitchen with more passion and love. We hope this book will encourage you to share these culinary creations with your friends and family.

Thank you for supporting this book, our community, and the entire KitchenKillaz family.

Bon Appétit

Acknowledgments

"I would like to thank my family and friends for their love and support over these last 7 years. This has been a dream of mine for a long time, and I am beyond thankful that I was able to team up with such a talented chef and work with such a phenomenal team. Thank you for inviting us into your homes, into your kitchens, and into your lives. I truly hope you enjoy this cookbook as much as we enjoyed making it. Bon Appétit !"

- Billy Floyd

"I would like to thank Sarah, Josh, my siblings, and my parents for always supporting me with my career and culinary endeavors. A special thanks goes out to Jay Moseley for giving me my love for cooking. I would also like to thank Billy for his friendship and support. The world is at its best when people can come together to enjoy music and food. The KitchenKillaz marries this beautifully and I am beyond thankful to be a part of it."

- Chef Dane Brevoort

Marketing

Donations

Thank you!

Notes

Notes

Printed in the USA
CPSIA information can be obtained
at www.ICGtesting.com
JSHW070803111224
75216JS00003B/10